Holiday Songs From Around the World
CHRISTMAS QUARTETS FOR ALL

Playable on ANY FOUR INS...
or any number of instruments...

WILLIAM RYDEN

TABLE OF CONTENTS

INSTRUMENTATION

EL9578 - Piano/Conductor, Oboe
EL9579 - Flute, Piccolo
EL9580 - Bb Clarinet, Bass Clarinet
EL9581 - Alto Saxophone (Eb Saxes and
         Eb Clarinets)
EL9582 - Tenor Saxophone
EL9583 - Bb Trumpet, Baritone T.C.

EL9584 - Horn in F
EL9585 - Trombone, Baritone B.C., Bassoon, Tuba
EL9586 - Violin
EL9587 - Viola
EL9588 - Cello/Bass
EL9589 - Percussion

Editor: Thom Proctor
Cover: Dallas Soto

ALPHABETICAL CONTENTS

WILLIAM RYDEN was born in New York City and is a life-long resident of Forest Hills, New York. He received his advanced musical training at The American Conservatory of Music in Chicago and at the Mannes College of Music in New York. The diversity of his composing ranges from solos to orchestra works, in both vocal and instrumental music. Since 1982 he has received 25 grants from the Meet-the-Composer Foundation. His numerous compositions and arrangements have been published by various prominent educational and performance music publishers.

WHILE SHEPHERDS WATCHED

FLUTE/PICCOLO

THOMAS ESTE'S PSALTER, 1592, England

WHILE BY MY SHEEP
(Echo Carol)

Germany

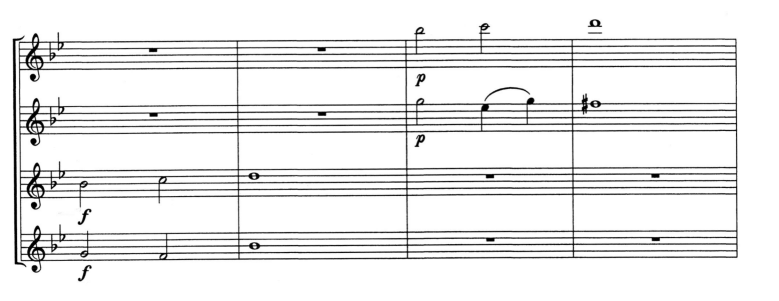

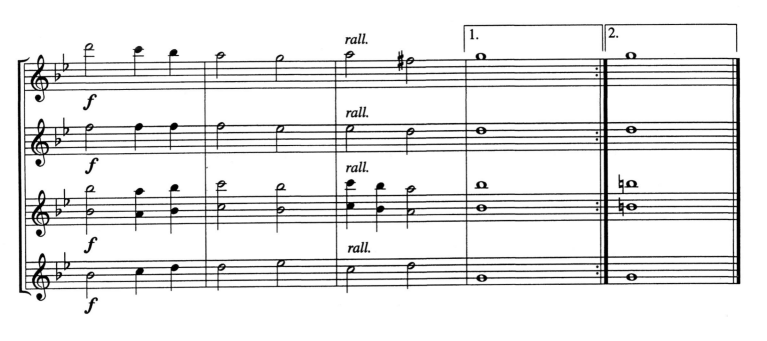

PUER NATUS
(A Child Was Born)

JOHANN SEBASTIAN BACH, Germany

AWAY IN A MANGER

WILLIAM JAMES KIRKPATRICK, America

LO, HOW A ROSE E'ER BLOOMING

Allegro moderato

MICHAEL PRAETORIUS, Germany

* 𝄐 = 𝅝

GLEE REIGNS IN GALILEE

Israel

HARK! THE HERALD ANGELS SING

FELIX MENDELSSOHN, Germany

IN DULCI JUBILO
(Now Sing We, Now Rejoice)

JOHANN SEBASTIAN BACH, Germany

DE TIERRA LEJANA VENIMOS
(Song of the Wise Men)

Puerto Rico

Andante con moto

WHAT CHILD IS THIS?

England

GOD REST YOU MERRY, GENTLEMEN

England

THE SHEPHERD'S FAREWELL
(from "L'enfance du Christ")

HECTOR BERLIOZ, France

GESU BAMBINO

Andante mosso

PIETRO ALESSANDRO YON, 1917, America

THE CROWN OF ROSES
"Legend"

PYOTR IL'YICH TCHAIKOVSKY, Russia

Moderato

COMPANIONS ALL SING LOUDLY

Basque